Looking Back at
Food
and Drink

SCHOOLHOUSE
PRESS

Original copyright © Macmillan Education Limited 1988

Author: Anne Mountfield

Editorial Planning by AMR

Designed and typeset by The Pen and Ink Book Company
Ltd, London

Illustrated by Trevor Ricketts and Patricia Capon

Picture Research by Liz Rudoff

Printed in Hong Kong

Library of Congress Cataloging-in-Publication Data

Looking back at food and drink.

   Includes index.
   Summary: Chronicles how humans have obtained
food through the ages, from hunting to harvesting
and explores how food is preserved, processed, and
flavored, and the different types of foods people
eat around the world. Also includes review questions
and a glossary.
   1. food--History--Juvenile literature. 2. Beverages--
History--Juvenile literature.   [1. Food--History]
TX355.L86 1988   641'.09   87-16414
ISBN 0-8086-1176-3
ISBN 0-8086-1183-6 (pbk.)

Photographic Credits

t=top b=bottom l=left r=right

The author and publishers wish to acknowledge
with thanks, the following photographic source
15, 20, 30*b*, 32, 38*t*, 41, 42 J Allan Cash, London;
13*l* Ardea, London; 34 BBC Hulton Picture
Library, London; 14 (Weidenfeld Archive), 33
Bodleian Library, Oxford; 6, 11*t*, 17*l*, 24
Bridgeman Art Library, London; 22 (Weidenfeld
Archive), 23*t* (Robert Harding Photograph
Library), 23*b* (Weidenfeld Archive), 25*r* (Robert
Harding Photograph Library) British Library,
London; contents (photograph Elisa Leonelli), 4
(photograph Doug Wilson), 8*r* (photograph
Farrell Grehan Wheeler), 9 (photograph Elisa
Leonelli), 17*r* (photograph Snowdon/Hoyer), 37
(photograph Gianni Tortoli), 43*b* (photograph
Cary Wolinsky) Colorific, London; 19*r* (Freer Art
Gallery, Washington DC), 25*l* E. T. Archive; 27,
29*b* Mary Evans Picture Library, London; 12, 16,
38*b* Sonia Halliday Photographs; 8*l*, 11*b*, 255, 28,
29*t*, 31, 35, 37*r* Robert Harding Photograph
Library, London; 5*t* and *b*, 7, 10, 27*t* Michael
Holford; 43*t* Hutchison Photograph Library,
London; 18, 19*l*, 36 Peter Neark's Western
Americana; 30*t* Picturepoint (UK); 13*r* Ronald
Sheridan Photographs; 39 (Byron Collection,
Museum of the City of New York) Weidenfeld
Archive

Cover illustration courtesy of the Bettmann
Archive, New York and BBC Hulton Picture
Library, London.

The publishers have made every effort to trace
the copyright holders, but if they have
inadvertently overlooked any, they will be
pleased to make the necessary arrangement at
the first opportunity.

Note to the reader
In this book there are some words in the text which are printed in **bold** type. This shows that the
word is listed in the glossary on page 46. The glossary gives a brief explanation of words which may
be new to you.

Contents

Introduction

▲ Families all over the world enjoy eating together, especially at festival times. This family in the United States is celebrating Thanksgiving. They are eating a special meal of turkey, with pumpkin pie for dessert. Thanksgiving Day is in November.

When you are hungry, it is a sign that your body wants some food. We have to eat to stay alive and to keep healthy. Food is something to enjoy also. Mealtimes bring groups of people together. Sharing food with someone else is also a way of showing friendship.

Today, many people can cook and enjoy food from all over the world. This book looks back at how farming, buying and selling, and **inventions** have made this possible.

The First Food Supplies

At first, people lived like other animals. They had to hunt for their food and they had to eat it raw. About 500,000 years ago, people first learned how to use fire for cooking. This meant that they could eat hot food. They could cook meat by putting the animals they killed into the hot ashes of the fire.

Then, about 15,000 years ago, people learned how to fish and how to trap birds for food. They started to keep their own animals and to grow their own plants. Sometimes, people grew too much of one thing and not enough of another. They began to **trade** with one another. All their food still came from the area in which they lived.

Three hundred years ago, sailors were already trading all over the world. New kinds of food and other goods began to reach Europe. The ships on this painted screen are Portuguese. They have arrived to trade in Japan.

Food from Other Countries

When people began to travel, they often brought back foods from the places they visited. Traders carried food over long distances on horseback or on camels. They charged high prices for these goods. Most people could only afford to buy the food and drink that was sold at nearby farms and markets.

About 1,000 years ago, people in Europe learned how to make strong sailing ships. They set out to look for other lands. These people took seeds and animals with them. Often, they found many things to eat that were unknown at home. They brought these new plants, fruits, and animals back to their own countries. Many of these plants and animals grew up and lived very well in their new countries.

▲ In the 1700's, the English traded with many countries. Different goods are being unloaded at this busy port in England.

Food Supplies Today

Today, food can be carried quickly across the world by road, air, or sea. In some countries, the towns and cities are full of food stores. Often, these countries grow more food than they need. There are other countries where people cannot grow enough food to feed themselves. Often, people in these countries are too poor to buy food from somewhere else. There are millions of people who do not have enough to eat. They are hungry every day of their lives.

From Hunting to Farming

In early times, people ate and drank the things that they could find near their homes. People drank water mostly, or sucked juicy fruit. They ate nuts and berries. They gathered the seeds, roots, and shoots of plants. They looked in the bark of trees for insects to eat. They found birds' eggs and bees' nests full of honey. They had to find out where wild plants were growing. People had to keep moving around. Sometimes, they could not find food for several days.

People also hunted animals for meat. Hunting animals was hard and often dangerous work. The people had to follow the herds of wild animals. At first, the hunters were armed only with rocks or with clubs. Soon, they learned how t make spears and axes from stone c wood. They made hunting nets by tyin together the stems of tough grasses. I some places, hollow stems of plants wer made into **blowpipes**. Sharp woode darts were blown through these pipe Later, people learned how to use meta to make knives and the tips of arrows.

Sowing Seeds

Some wild grass seeds, or **grains**, ar useful foods. They can be stored for us in the winter. People collected grain t **grind** into flour. The flour was mixe with water and baked in an oven or pot.

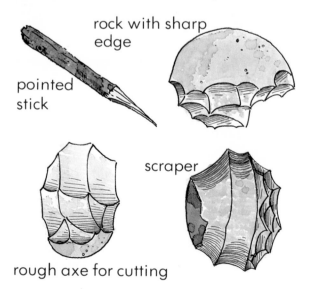

rock with sharp edge

pointed stick

scraper

rough axe for cutting

▲ The first hunters made their own weapons. They made spears and arrows with pointed sticks. They used sharp stones to make tools for cutting.

▲ People have been sowing grain crops for thousands of years. This is a farmer in the 1400's. He is sowing wheat by throwing handfuls of seed over the field.

Then, people found out that they did [no]t need to travel around so much. They [co]uld plant seeds near their homes and [ha]rvest them. If they saved some seed, [th]ey could grow more grain again the [ne]xt year. People lived and worked [to]gether in groups. They **settled** in one [pl]ace and began to live as farmers.

[K]eeping Flocks and Herds

About 10,000 years ago, in the Middle [Ea]st, hunters discovered a new way to [ge]t meat. Instead of hunting wild [an]imals, people could tame them and [ke]ep them close to their homes. They [m]ade their homes near grassy lands so [th]at their flocks and herds could graze.

Sometimes, people grew grain to feed their animals in the winter. Sheep and goats were some of the first animals to be kept near the home. Pigs, cows, and hens were the next animals to be kept on farms.

At first, the animals were kept just for their meat. Then, people learned how to use the milk of their animals to make cheese. Like grain, cheese could be stored and eaten in the winter months. People no longer needed to hunt.

▼ This picture was painted in ancient Egypt more than 3,000 years ago. Cattle like these can still be seen in Africa. The Egyptians used cattle to provide milk, just as we do today.

Food from Animals

In some places, the farmers kept only animals. Today, there are still people who live like this. The Masai people of Kenya, in East Africa, keep cows, but they do not grow any food. They travel to find grass for their herds. Other farmers grow plant foods, or **crops**, and keep animals as well. Some of their crops are used as food for their animals.

Farmers around the world keep many types of animals. They can keep sheep and cows where there is grass. Goats and llamas can live on stony hillsides. Camels can live in areas that are very hot and dry. Camels can go for weeks without drinking any water.

▲ This Masai woman in Kenya is milking a cow. The milk is mixed with cows' blood to make a nourishing drink. This drink is an important food for the Masai people.

Meat in the Winter

At first, the only way to get fresh me in the winter was to hunt. People hunte many wild animals, such as bears, wi pigs, deer, and rabbits. Even when the started farming, people still had to hur in the winter. In cold, norther countries, grasses do not grow in th winter. In the past, farmers could n grow very much food. They could n feed their animals all through the yea Each autumn, they killed off most o their herd. They kept only a few anima alive. They used these animals to bree more animals. The animals' offsprin would make up the next year's herd.

▲ This man is a Saami. The Saami live in Lapland where it is very cold. They keep large herds of reindeer. They use these animals for their meat, milk, and hides.

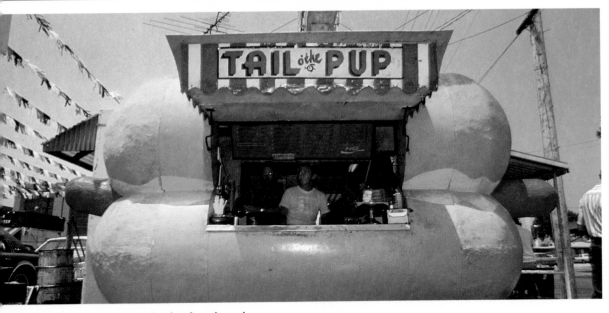

This is a "hot dog" stand. The first hot dog appeared in 1893. A food seller in the United States sold hot sausages in a roll, in order to make them easy to hold. There is a German dog called a dachshund which is often called a "sausage dog." Someone drew a cartoon of one in a roll. This is how hot dogs got their name.

Rules for Eating Meat

Sometimes, eating meat can make people sick. If the meat is not fresh, it can spoil very quickly. Some groups of people began to have rules about eating meat. People began to think that some kinds of meat are "unclean." Often, these meats are the ones that spoil very quickly. Jews do not eat pork. All their meat must be drained of blood so that it keeps fresher. Then, it is called **kosher** meat.

The Muslim religion also made rules about how meat must be killed and handled. Meat prepared in the Muslim way is called **halal**. Muslims do not eat pork either.

Keeping and Cooking Meat

Until about 150 years ago, there were no refrigerators or cold storage to keep meat fresh. In hot weather, it quickly began to spoil and smell. However, there were some ways to keep, or **preserve**, meat for months. People could dry it by leaving it in the sun, or by packing it in salt. Often, the meat was tough. The animals were small, and they did not have much fat. Fat helps to make the meat tender and keeps it from drying out when it is cooked. Often, the meat did not taste very good after it had been preserved. Cooks began to invent sauces to make the meat more tender and better-tasting.

One way of using dried meat was to make sausages. Sausages have been made for a very long time. They were made in Babylon over 3,000 years ago. They were made from chopped, salted meat. This was packed into tubes from an animal's intestines.

Birds for Food

The first hunters caught birds easily with nets and traps. At first, most birds were kept for their eggs. The birds were not used for meat until they were old.

Eggs have always been a cheap kind of food. They were eaten daily. Bird meat, or **poultry**, was eaten only at special times. In the last fifty years, new ways of farming poultry and keeping the meat fresh have been found. These have made poultry cheaper than ever before. Also, poultry has less fat than other types of meat and this has made it more popular.

▲ The Egyptians hunted many birds in the marshes along the Nile. The hunter in this painting is using a cat to help him hunt.

Ducks and Geese

Wild ducks and geese are found in many parts of the world. In China, they have been caught and bred for food for thousands of years. In many other places, large duck eggs are eaten. Ducks and geese were kept for their feathers, as well as for their eggs and meat. The feathers were used to make feather beds. The wing feathers of geese were used as pens. Until about 200 years ago, geese were often eaten at Christmas in Europe.

Before the railroads were built, flocks of geese were herded from the countryside to many big cities a few weeks before Christmas. They had to walk for many miles. The geese were kept in warehouses and fed until they were fat. Then, they were ready for the Christmas table. Geese are still eaten in some of the countries in the north of Europe.

Chickens and Turkeys

Wild chickens came from the forests of Asia and were bred there first. They were brought from Asia to Europe over 2,000 years ago. Chickens were kept for their meat and their eggs. In ancient Rome, people often gave chickens as gifts to the **temples**. The priests killed the chickens and offered them to the gods as food.

Wild turkeys were found in North and South America. People in Mexico started to breed them. The Spanish came to Mexico. They took some turkeys with them when they returned to Europe.

In the United States, turkey is the traditional meal eaten on Thanksgiving. On the first Thanksgiving, the Native American Chief Massasoit gave turkeys to the Pilgrims to help celebrate the success of their first harvest. Today, Americans eat turkey on Thanksgiving Day just as the Pilgrims did more than 360 years ago.

Wild Birds

In the past, people ate many wild birds, such as swans, peacocks, crows, larks and thrushes. Kings and queens sometimes ate fancy dishes made with humming birds. Today, in some places, there are laws to keep these birds from being killed.

Other wild birds, such as pheasant and grouse, can only be killed at certain times of the year. They cannot be killed during the breeding season, so that the populations of these birds will remain at safe levels.

In Europe, goose used to be the most widely eaten bird at feasts. The turkey became more popular after it was taken to Europe from America in the 1500's.

▼ The ostrich is the biggest of all birds. It cannot fly, but it can run very fast. This man on horseback is chasing the bird. He is using a rope with a heavy ball on each end. They are called bolas. Ostrich meat is not eaten very much today.

Fish as Food

▲ Fishing has always been dangerous and difficult. This picture shows fishermen about 1,500 years ago. Today, fishermen still use nets, but they have stronger boats and machinery to help them.

Fish is another kind of food that has been eaten since early times. In some places, fish are caught in the sea. In other places, they come from fresh water such as rivers or lakes.

Early people used thorns tied to the end of a tough grass line. Also, they used hooks carved out of animal bones to catch river fish. Sometimes, they shot the fish with arrows. In the Middle East, fishing rods with lines were used almost 3,000 years ago. In ancient Egypt, people caught fish with nets or spears. Farther south, on African rivers, fishermen made traps to catch fish.

There are many kinds of fish. Differe[nt] kinds live in different parts of the worl[d.] Early settlers in America found a lot [of] cod off the coast of Massachusetts. Th[e] area from which the cod fishing boats s[et] out has been called Cape Cod ever sinc[e.]

Fishing in the Sea

Most fishing in the sea is done fro[m] small boats by the people who live alon[g] the coast. The way in which the fish a[re] caught depends on where the people liv[e] in the world. In China and Japan, peop[le] use large diving birds called cormorant[s.] For over 1,000 years, these birds hav[e] been trained to catch fish. In India an[d] China, some boats have nets attached t[o] the end of poles. The poles work like [a] seesaw. The end with the net is dippe[d] into the water. Then, it is pulled up t[o] see if there are any fish in the net.

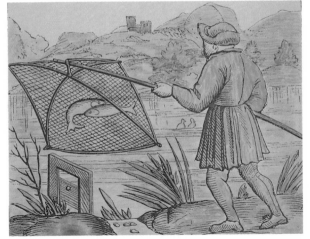

Cormorants are related to pelicans. In China
d Japan, fishermen tame cormorants. The
ermen attach a ring around the cormorant's
:k and get it to dive into the sea to catch fish.
 ring keeps the cormorant from swallowing
 fish. The cormorant is allowed to eat every
h fish. This photograph was taken in China.

▲ It is best to keep fish alive until they are ready
to eat. This is a fishpond from about 300 years
ago. People stored fish in enclosed ponds like
this one. In some places, there are still fish
farms, where large numbers of fish are kept in
ponds.

People learned how to build bigger
d stronger boats. Then, they could fish
 waters that were a long way from the
ast. Many fishermen use a very large,
g-shaped net. The net is dragged along
e bed of the sea by either one or two
ats. This is called **trawling**. Hundreds
 fish can be caught at the same time in a
awler's big net.

Often, trawlers go a long way from
nd. They do not return for days or
eeks. The fish that are caught by the
awlers have to be kept fresh. Some
ats store the fish in packs of ice. Other
ats store the fish in cans. The cans are
ghtly sealed. **Canning** the fish keeps it
om spoiling. The boats which are able
 freeze or can large amounts of fish at
a are very big.

Eating Fish

In some places, fish makes up the main
part of people's food. Often, fish takes
the place of meat in these parts of the
world. The food in Japan is mainly fish.
Often, it is eaten raw. It is called *sushi*.
The Romans ate many kinds of fish. We
know this from patterns drawn on the
plates and dishes that they used. These
pictures show many kinds of fish. The
Romans used a fish paste, called **garum**,
to flavor their cooking. Garum was made
from dried salted fish.

About a hundred years ago, in Britain,
shops selling cooked fish were opened.
The fish was sold hot and eaten with
bread. People usually ate this take-out
meal in the streets. Later, fish was sold
with French fried potatoes.

Milk as Food

Animals such as cows, goats, and sheep were first kept for their skins and their meat. Then, people began to drink their milk. It took thousands of years for people to learn how to store milk without it turning sour. In some countries, camels, buffaloes, and reindeer are milked. Milk, and foods that are made from milk, are called **dairy foods**.

People in Turkey found a way to thicken milk into a food called **yogurt**.

▲ People have kept cows for milk for thousands of years. Milking was always done by hand up until about eighty years ago. The first milking machine was invented in 1878 by an American woman named Anna Baldwin. Milking machines went on sale in 1918. They were designed by a Swedish man named Carl de Laval. Today, farms with many cows use milking machines.

Sometimes, they mixed the yogurt with little cucumber, melon, or dried fru This could be eaten with meat dishes, by itself. People in the United States a Britain have eaten yogurt only for the la forty years. In other places, like t Middle East and the USSR, it has be popular for thousands of years.

Cheese

Cheese has been made since ear times. We know that cheese was mac and eaten in ancient Greece and Rom When milk is no longer fresh, it ca separate into two parts. The thick part called **curds**. The curds are full of protei and fat. The **whey** is watery and thi People learned how to use the curds make cheese. The ways of making chees have changed very little. To mak cheese, the curds are pressed togethe so that the whey runs out. This leaves solid mass of curd. A hard cheese made when the curd is pressed betwee boards for many days. Then, the chees can be stored for months.

Some countries have a famous chees The Netherlands is known for its Goud and Edam. Britain is known for its Stilto and Cheddar. Greece is known for i Fetta cheese. Cheeses taste different because they are made from the milk different animals. Cows' milk, goat milk, and sheep's milk are the mo widely used. About 400 years ag France became famous for its cheese There are hundreds of French cheese Often, they are named after the village area where they are made, lik Roquefort.

14

This is a famous cheese market in Alkmaar in e Netherlands. The market is held each Friday, through the summer. The cheeses are carried boat-shaped pallets. Porters in colorful hats ad the cheese onto the trucks and barges.

utter and Cream

The part of the milk which contains the ost fat is called the cream. Butter is ade by beating, or **churning**, cream. rt of the cream drains away as a liquid. nis liquid is called buttermilk. Part of e cream turns into solid butterfat. This the butter. In the past, the cream was aten in a large wooden tub called a tter churn. Today, butter is churned machine in factories.

In America and most countries in orthern Europe, butter has been used r a long time. In Africa and India, cooks sed a kind of oily butter called **ghee**. ften, ghee is made from buffalo milk. me countries did not use butter. They sed oil and animal fat for cooking.

▲ Butter always used to be made by hand. The cream was put in a barrel called a churn. A handle was turned to make wooden paddles inside the churn move. These beat the cream, so that it became butter.

Tools for Growing Food

About 6,000 years ago, farmers broke up the ground with sticks and sharp stones. Later, farmers used **hoes** made of simple materials. Some were made of wood with sharp stones attached. Others were made of animal horns. The hoes were used to clear away loose stones and weeds. Then, the seeds were sown in the ground.

People started to use larger tools which were pulled by animals. In ancient Egypt, oxen were strapped together. They pulled a large wooden digging tool behind them. This would break up the hard, dry earth. The tool was like a plow. Later, plows were made with wheels, so that they could run over the ground more easily. These plows could turn the soil over, as well as break it up. The use of animals meant that more ground could be broken up and more seeds could be sown.

▲ This picture shows Egyptains harvesting crop about 3,000 years ago. The curved knives they are using are called sickles. Today, sickles are still used in many places for cutting crops.

Planting and Harvesting

About 200 years ago, many new farming machines were made. Jethro Tu invented a machine called a seed dri which sowed seeds in rows. Then, plant could be weeded easily. Until a hundre years ago, crops had always been cut b hand. Large, curved knives, calle **sickles**, were used. The crop wa collected and beaten with sticks, o **threshed**. This separates the grain from the stalk.

▶ After the crop is cut, the grains must be removed. The farmer is beating the wheat with a flail. This was a hinged stick. It made it easier to separate the grain from the stalk. Beating the crop is still done in many parts of the world.

hen, machines were invented to cut, **reap**, the crops. One of these chines could do the work of many ple. They were used first in the ited States to take the places of the ny men who left the farms to look for d. In Britain, the reaping machines led fights in the streets. The machines re taking the farm workers' jobs. day, many farms use **combine rvesting** machines. These can cut the in and thresh it. These machines are y big. They have a place to store the in as they cut the crop. The left-over aw is thrown out onto the field in les.

Mills

The seeds of many grains can be ground to make flour for bread. Often, the seeds of wheat and corn are used. Grinding the seeds makes a fine powder out of the tough grain. One of the earliest ways to grind grain was to spread the seeds on a large flat stone. Another stone was placed on top. People or animals turned the stone on top around and around. The turning stone ground the seeds into flour.

For about 800 years, windmills have been used to make flour. The mills were built on hills, so that the wind could turn their sails. The turning sails moved the **millstones**. The heavy millstones turned and ground the grain into flour. Today, most of the world's flour is ground by huge electric machines.

▲ Windmills have been used for a long time. This one is in Denmark. The wind turns the sails of the windmill. The turning sails move two millstones inside the mill. The grain is ground between the stones.

Grains

▲ Huge amounts of wheat grow in the United States and Canada. This farm is in northern Texas. There is wheat growing as far as the eye can see. Very large combine harvesters have to be used to harvest so much grain.

Plants which give us grain have been grown by farmers for thousands of years. The grain seeds can be boiled until they are soft, or ground into flour. Often, grain plants are called **cereals**.

In most countries, one grain food is eaten every day. This is called the **staple** food. Different grains grow better in different climates. Wheat and corn are staple foods in cool climates. Rice is the staple food in Southeast Asia. Young rice plants have to have heavy rainfall which comes at certain times of the year in these areas.

Wheat

Wheat has been grown and eaten for a long time. Grains of wheat were buried with the kings of ancient Egypt. The Egyptians thought the kings would need the wheat for food on the journey to heaven. About 4,500 years ago, traders from the Middle East were selling wheat to India and China. Later, wheat was found to grow well in Europe. It was a good grain to store because it did not rot easily.

The early settlers who came to North America from Europe planted wheat. The wheat grew very well. The settlers started to sell wheat and flour to France. Other countries, such as Canada and Australia, started to grow wheat, also.

orn

Corn was first grown by the Inca people of South America. Later, it was own by the Native Americans. In 1492, e explorer Christopher Columbus ached North America. Here, his men w fields of corn for the first time. They ok corn seed back with them, and anted it in Europe.

Some of the early settlers in the United ates almost starved to death. They ere saved by Native Americans. They owed the settlers how to plant the corn d how to grind it into flour. A Native merican named Squanto showed the ilgrims how to heat corn seeds until ey burst. This made popcorn. The hole ear of corn can be boiled also. This called "corn on the cob." Today, many reakfast cereals are made from corn. hey are made in factories.

Rice

Almost half of the people in the world eat rice as their staple food. Rice grows best when the fields are flooded with water. It is grown in places where there is plenty of rain and plenty of sunshine. Rice grows quickly, and can ripen in three months. Sometimes, it is possible to have two harvests in a year.

Rice was grown in India and China about 5,000 years ago. Later, it was brought to Europe. Today, it is grown in parts of Italy. Over 300 years ago, rice was planted in South Carolina. The rice grew well in the local soil. By 1893, South Carolina had become an important center for rice-growing. Today, the United States is one of the world's major exporters of rice.

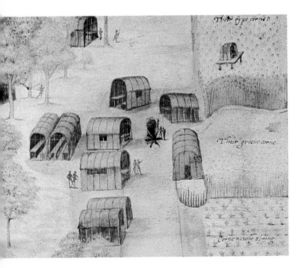

▲ Wheat was not always grown in North America. Before Europeans arrived there, the Native Americans grew corn. This picture shows ornfields in a Native American village in North Carolina in the 1600's.

▲ People in the Far East have been growing rice for thousands of years. Rice needs plenty of water while it is growing. The people had to work hard to get water into the rice fields.

Vegetables

Vegetables are the parts of leafy plants that are eaten. Sometimes, they are eaten raw. Sometimes, they may be cooked by themselves, or added to soups, stews, and sauces. The part that is eaten may be a root like a carrot. It may be a stem like asparagus, or a bulb like an onion. Leaves, such as cabbage and lettuce, are also vegetables. The seeds, such as peas, or the flowers, such as cauliflower, are eaten as vegetables also. Some fruits that are not sweet are often considered to be vegetables. Avccados, peppers, and tomatoes are all fruit-vegetables.

▼ People have always enjoyed eating green vegetables. They like to buy many different kinds of vegetables. This market stand is selling a wide variety of vegetables.

Early people in Europe and Asia foun vegetables like peas, beans, onion: garlic, leeks, and cabbage growing wilc All these were eaten in Roman time: The Romans grew many other types c vegetables in their gardens. They grev beets, zucchinis, pumpkins, and turnips Sometimes, the vegetables were boiled i water or they were cooked in olive oil.

▼ Both onions and garlic have strong flavors. The Egyptians thought they were symbols of the world and new life. They put them in the pyramids with the dead. In Europe, people believed that garlic would keep evil away. Many people still believe that garlic is good for them.

◀ Seeds such as peas and beans are called pulses. Pulses are especially good for us. They contain protein, which we all need to stay strong and healthy. Pulses can be dried easily and stored for a long time.

Potatoes

Potatoes, pumpkins, and lima beans are all vegetables that first grew in South America. The Spanish explorers first saw potatoes in Peru over 400 years ago. They took them back to Europe.

At first, potatoes were not liked in Europe. The French people thought that they were poisonous. The King of France wanted country people to grow them. The King thought up a plan. He ordered his gardeners to plant some potatoes. When the potatoes grew up to be plants, the king ordered his soldiers to guard them. At night, the soldiers were sent home. People thought potatoes must be good if the king had his plants guarded. Some people crept out at night and stole the potatoes. Then, they began to plant potatoes themselves. Potatoes became the main food for many country people in Europe after that.

Vegetables in Hot Countries

In the past, vegetables that had been cooked were often safer to eat than meat or fish that was not fresh. This is still true in hot countries. Often, people eat little or no meat. Often, root plants like **cassava** are the staple food. Sweet potatoes, or **yams**, are eaten widely in many African countries, in the West Indies, and the southern part of the United States.

Most people in Europe ate root vegetables, such as carrots or turnips. Farmers found that they could make the soil in fields better by growing root crops in them. During the winter, some root crops were used as animal food. Until about 400 years ago, most people could only eat the vegetables that grew near where they lived. Then, the traders brought foods back from the places that they visited. At first, they brought back root crops because these kept longer. The first carrots were brought to Europe from Afghanistan. They were purple. Carrots were thought to be so unusual that ladies wore the feathery green tops pinned to their hats.

Fruit

▲ Apples have been a favorite fruit for thousands of years. The Greeks and the Romans grew several different kinds of apples. In this apple orchard from the 1200's, some people are picking the fruit. Others are cutting down old trees and planting new ones.

In the past, people picked the wild berries and nuts that grew near where they lived. Over the years, they learned how to grow their own trees by planting the seeds of these fruits. Fields of fruit trees are called **orchards**.

People learned to keep bees next to the fruit orchards. The bees spread the grains of **pollen** from the flowers so that all the trees gave fruit. The bees gave a supply of honey, too. The Romans used honey as a sweetener. They did not have any sugar.

Also, the Romans kept apples, figs, plums, pears, and cherries packed in honey. The honey kept the fruit, so that it could be eaten during the winter when fruit does not grow.

Fruit from Different Climates

Some fruits, like apples and pears, grow well in cool weather. Plenty of water is needed for the trees to grow. The trees also need some sunshine, so that the fruit can ripen. Small apples, called crab apples, have grown for thousands of years in most European countries. The Romans took apples to Britain. Many hundreds of years later, the British took the apples to North America. Now, there are very many types of apples growing in different areas.

Some fruits, such as dates and pineapples, grow only in hot countries. Bananas grow mainly in very hot, wet climates, which are called the **tropics**. Pineapples are a tropical plant, too.

When fruits from hot countries first arrived in Europe, it was expensive to buy them. Today, many kinds of fruit are shipped quickly all over the world by air or by sea. Fresh fruit can be bought all through the year in many countries. The fruit has been grown in a country or area with a different climate.

Oranges and Lemons

Oranges and lemons contain a lot of citric acid, so they are called citrus fruits. Citrus fruits contain a lot of **vitamin C**. People need vitamin C to keep healthy. Limes and grapefruit are citrus fruits also. Oranges were grown by the Chinese at least 3,000 years ago. They were taken to Europe by explorers and traders. About 300 years ago, oranges were often sold in the European theaters, in the same way as popcorn is today.

Today, oranges and lemons are grown in many parts of the world. They are grown in the United States, the Middle East, South Africa, and the warmer parts of Europe. From these places, they are shipped throughout the world for people to enjoy.

▲ This is a grocery store in London about 200 years ago. The fruit and vegetables were things grown mainly in Britain. Fruit from abroad, such as pineapples, was very expensive.

These are Persians who lived about 1,000 years ago. They are eating pomegranates. These fruits first grew in Iran, which was once called Persia. People thought that eating these fruits would cure people of envy and hatred.

What Do People Drink?

All of us must have water in order to stay alive. People have always used water to drink and for washing. The water had to be collected from rivers, wells, and springs. People carried the water to their homes in buckets, or in jars. Some people collected rain water.

Drinking water must be clean. Dirty water is full of tiny living things called **germs**. The germs can make people very sick. Over 2,000 years ago, the Romans knew how to bring clean water by pipes to their towns. They also learned how to store water in large tanks, or **cisterns**. From there, the water was piped to some big houses and street fountains. Later, people allowed the Roman water systems to become ruins. They went back to collecting and drinking water from rivers, wells, and springs for hundreds of years. In many parts of the world, water is still collected in this way.

Beer and Wine

Often, water was a dangerous drink until people learned to store it and clean it. Instead of water, most people, including children, drank some kind of alcohol. The alcohol was made by adding grain, sugar, and **yeast** to boiled water. Yeast helps the sugar and grain to turn into alcohol. The alcohol helped to keep the drink free from germs. Later, people came to know that too much alcohol is not good for our bodies.

▲ This picture shows a wine festival in Belgium over 300 years ago. The juice is pressed out of the grapes by screwing down the wine press.

Until 500 years ago, ale was the main drink in northern Europe. Ale was made from a cereal called barley, with honey, sugar, and yeast added. When a plant called **hops**, was added to ale, the drink became known as beer.

Another drink that was popular was wine. This was mainly made and drunk in southern Europe. Wine is made from grapes. Early settlers from Europe planted grape plants, or **vines**, in North and South America. The wine was stored in bottles. Later, people realized that the wine would keep for a long time if the bottles were sealed with corks. Today there are many types of grapes grown in different areas. These grapes are made into many wines which have different tastes.

ea and Coffee

Tea is made by adding hot water to the ied leaves of the tea plant. In China d Japan, tea has been drunk for ousands of years. It was first taken to rope about 300 years ago. A cup of cha," as it was called, was very pensive. People kept the tea leaves cked up in tea jars, called **tea caddies**. here are many different kinds of tea, d many ways to drink it, too. Some ople drink tea with milk added to it. me people put a slice of lemon into eir tea. In India, the people often add ices to their tea.

In Japan, there is a ceremony when tea is rved. The tea is made very slowly. Each action done in a special way. This picture shows a tea remony from the 1900's.

Coffee was grown first in Ethiopia in Africa. Later, it was grown and used widely in the Middle East. At first, coffee beans were ground up and mixed with a fat. Then, coffee beans were eaten. Later, coffee was used as a medicine. Then, it was used as a drink. In 1652, in London, a Turkish trader opened a shop where people could go to drink coffee. It was called a coffee house. Coffee houses became popular all over Europe. Now, coffee is drunk all over the world. In the United States, people drink coffee first thing in the morning or after meals.

▼ Coffee houses were once a popular place for people to meet. In the 1700's, there were more than 2,000 coffee houses in London. The coffee was drunk without milk, and served in little bowls.

Ways of Cooking

Each village might have one oven, which all the people shared. It was filled with firewood. The firewood burned away, and the walls stayed hot. Bread could then be baked in the oven.

To cook food means to heat it. After has been heated, it may be eaten hot cold. Cooking changes the taste of food Boiling food in water can make it sof Roasting it over a fire or baking it in a h oven can make it crisp.

Cooking on an Open Fire

The first food to be cooked wa probably meat. The meat may have bee cooked first by accident, when some fe into an open fire. People found that th roasted meat tasted good. The meat wa pushed onto a stick and held over th fire. Later, meat was hung on a meta pole that was set up over the flames. Thi is called **spit** roasting.

▼ This is part of the famous Bayeux tapestry. This tapestry was made to tell about William of Normandy's conquest of England in 1066. Here we can see soldiers cooking meat over a fire on spit. Today, we call this sort of cooking a barbecue.

Before people had cooking pots, they
used earth ovens to cook food. They dug
a hole in the ground, and lined it with
stones. Next, they lit a fire at the bottom.
They let the fire burn until the stones
were hot. Then, they dropped the meat
onto the stones. They covered the top of
the hole with grasses and earth. The
meat cooked in the hot air below.

In early times, most cooking took place
out of doors. Often, the ovens or the
cooking areas were some distance from
people's homes. This was to keep the
huts from catching fire.

Cooking

The first cooking pots were made from
stone or tree bark. Clay pots were first
made about 8,500 years ago. These pots
could be put close to the fire, or in an
oven. If they were put on the flames,
they cracked. It was many thousands of
years before metal cooking pots were
made.

Metal pots were used for boiling water
and for cooking soups and stews. They
were called **cauldrons**. Cauldrons often
stood on three-legged stands over the
fire. Sometimes small pots were placed
inside the cauldron to cook small
amounts of food. Bread was sometimes
cooked in metal pots with lids. These
were called **bake ovens**.

This picture shows a kitchen range from about
200 years ago. The fire heated the ovens at the
side. Bread and cakes were baked in the ovens.
The meat was cooked by hanging it in front of
the fire.

Fireplaces and Ovens

Hundreds of years ago in Europe, the
kitchen fire was used both for cooking
and for heating. Cauldrons hung on
chains over large log fires. A metal spit
was set up over the fire for roasting meat.
Some spits in large kitchens were big
enough to hold a whole sheep or cow.
Sometimes, a bread oven was built into
the wall beside the hot fire.

About 300 years ago, coal started to be
burned instead of logs. Coal takes up less
space than logs, so fireplaces became
smaller. Then, closed metal stoves, or
ranges, were built into the open
fireplace.

Then, people learned how to use gas
for cooking. The first gas stoves were
sold about a hundred years ago. The gas
was made in power plants. It was sent
through underground pipes to the
stoves. The flow of the gas was not very
even. Often, the gas stoves exploded.
Later, electric stoves were made. They
were safer, but at first they took a long
time to heat up and to cool down.

Baking

Baking is a way of cooking food to make it dry out. No extra water or fat is used. Baking is done in a closed oven or on a hot, dry surface. Baked bread has been a staple food for many people for hundreds of years.

Bread was made by mixing flour with water and baking it dry. The way to make bread has changed very little since people learned how to make flour. The flour can be made from wheat, **rye**, corn, oats, or other grain. The color and taste of bread depends on the flour that is used to bake it. Bread made from rye is very dark and sometimes black. Bread made from corn is yellow. Whole-wheat bread is brown.

White bread is made from flour that has been **sifted**. This means that the darker outside part of the grain has been taken out. This took a long time to do. For a very long time, white bread was very expensive. Today, it is often less expensive than wheat or rye bread.

There are different kinds of bread. Sometimes, the flour and water are mixed with yeast to make the bread rise. This bread must be baked in an oven. Other kinds of bread do not have yeast in them and are flat. They can be baked in a pan on the fire. Indian **chappattis** are flat breads of this kind. Often, flat breads and thick slices of risen bread were used as plates. Sometimes, cheese or onions were added to the meal to give flavour.

▲ In Mexico, people make a kind of flat bread called a tortilla. Tortillas are made from cornmeal. They are cooked on a metal or clay griddle. Often, people eat them with a spicy meat sauce.

Cakes

Sometimes, honey or sugar was added to the flour and water to make cakes. The first cakes were sweetened with honey. Usually, they were eaten at special festivals. Jews make cakes just before their feast of the **Passover**. The cakes use up all the old flour that has been bought in the time before Passover. On Christmas Eve, in Germany, people eat cakes and cookies that are baked with honey and ginger spice.

Cakes often have other kinds of flour in them like ground almonds or ground rice. In Italy, at Easter, people bake cakes made with almond paste. Sometimes dried fruit is added to the cake mixture. Cake like this is often eaten at weddings and at Christmas in Britain.

Pastries and Pies

Pastry is a mixture of fat and flour. It is used to wrap around meat or cooked fruit to make a pie. Hot pies have been popular in colder countries for many years. Some pies contain meat or vegetables. Some have fruit and spices in them.

At feasts in the past, cooks in Europe sometimes put live animals, like birds and frogs, into pies. This was done as a joke.

In many countries, cooks invented their own pastry recipes. Austrian cooks, for example, are proud of their very thin **strudel** pastry. They like it to be so thin that "one can read an old love letter through it." The strudel is stuffed with apple, raisins, or cream cheese.

People eat cakes on special occasions. This man is decorating a wedding cake with sugar icing. The sugar is mixed with the white of eggs to make the icing hard. Icing can be made into beautiful shapes like these shells and the fish on top. The man has made the cake look like a fountain.

Pies have been popular for hundreds of years. This picture was drawn in the 1850's. The cook is putting the pastry cover on top of a pie. The pie may contain meat, or it may contain fruit, such as apples or cherries.

Food from Other Countries

In the past, people ate food that came from nearby farms or local markets. Local dishes depended on whether people lived near the sea or inland. Local crops, fruit, and animals were eaten. Very little food was brought from faraway lands.

Ways of Eating

In China, Japan, and Malaysia, rice is a staple food. Often, it is eaten with dishes of other foods. Meat, fish, and vegetables are cut into strips. Then, they are cooked for a very short time in hot oil or in boiling water. Many dishes of food are served at the same time. The rice and other foods are eaten from small bowls. Two long sticks, called **chopsticks**, are used to eat with. The chopsticks are squeezed together to pick up the food.

In some countries, everyone eats from one big dish. In other countries, people put their food on a leaf or on a piece of bread. In many places, bread is used to scoop up the food. In some countries, food is eaten only with the right hand. All over the world, it is usual to kneel or sit on the floor to eat. In Europe, in the past, people usually sat on chairs or benches at a high table. This custom has spread to many other parts of the world.

▲ This Ethiopian family is eating a hot spicy di called wat. They are eating the wat on large pieces of flat bread, called injera. It is so large covers the whole table. The family breaks off pieces of injera to pick up the wat.

▶ In Japan, people eat from small bowls and they use chopsticks. This couple are having a picnic. They are using a small table. This is also traditional in Japan.

ocal Foods

Most countries have favorite local ods. In India, food is cooked with eds and spices. Some of these spices e very strong. A lot of people in India not eat meat. They think that it is rong to kill animals. These people are **getarians**. They eat vegetables and ntils with rice or flat bread.

In countries with seacoasts, people ually eat a lot of fish. In Sweden and orway, herrings that have been soaked salt water or vinegar are a favorite od. On the eastern coast of the United ates, people make a thick soup from ams and other seafood. It is called a nowder. Often, Japanese families eat eir fish raw. Only very fresh fish can be sed. Usually, it is served with seaweed. he Japanese eat several kinds of aweed.

Food for Special Occasions

Every country has special foods that are eaten at special times of the year. Indian children like the sweet foods that are eaten at the festival of Diwali. In Australia, it is hot and sunny in December. Often, Christmas dinner is a barbecue cooked on the beach. The New Year food in Japan is made from a mixture of rice and water. This is beaten into a paste and eaten. It is called **mochi**.

Today, in many cities and towns, there are people who have come from other parts of the world. Often, they open stores or restaurants to sell their own types of food. A family in the United States may try raw fish and rice in the Japanese style. At the same moment, a Japanese family in Tokyo may be eating an American-style hamburger.

Sometimes, people like a ange from the traditional od of their own country. his is a fast-food restaurant Japan. Fast-food staurants started in the nited States, but they can w be found all over the orld.

Flavoring Food

Many people used to eat the same kind of food all the time. Often, the food was not very fresh so it did not taste very nice. Therefore, spices and herbs were used to make the food taste different. Honey or sugar was used to sweeten it.

Salt and Pepper

From early times, salt was very precious. It was used to add flavor to food and to help keep food from spoiling. Salt can be dug out of the ground or made from sea water. Roman soldiers were given salt as part of their pay. The word "salary" really means "an allowance of salt."

Often, strong-smelling and strong-tasting spices were used to hide the taste of meat or fish that was not very fresh. In Europe, spices were very expensive. They had to be brought over long distances by traders. Most of the spices grew only in hot countries. They came from Asia and the Middle East.

In some countries, such as Sri Lanka, Mexico, and South America, the people like to eat their food cooked with strong, hot spices like **chili**. In other countries, they like to use spices that are not so hot. Some spices, like **cinnamon**, are thought to be good for the health. Pepper is used all over the world to flavor food. Peppercorns were also used as a form of money at one time. A very small rent is still called a peppercorn rent.

▲ We use spices to make our food more tasty. Many spices are grown in hot countries. This market is in Nigeria. The women are selling hot red peppers and a yellow powder called turmeric.

Herbs

Small green plants, like basil, thyme, and mint, are called herbs. Herbs have leaves with a strong smell. The dried leaves have been used to flavor food for a long time. The smell or taste of these plants comes from the oil in the leaves.

Over 200 years ago, it was common to grow herbs in a special herb garden. People used herbs as medicine. They made herbal drinks, such as mint tea, which they drank when they were sick. Today, some people still prefer to use herbs as medicine.

Sweeteners

For thousands of years, honey was the only sweetener known in Europe. It was used to sweeten cakes and drinks. Honey was used for medicines also. Over 2,000 years ago, the Roman people offered honey cakes in their temples to please their gods.

Most sugar comes from long, tall plants called **sugarcane**. Sugarcane is crushed in a mill until the sweet juice comes out of the plant. Then, the juice is boiled. The sugar turns into **crystals**, and leaves a dark, sticky syrup. The syrup is called **molasses**. For a long time, the sugar crystals were sold in a cone-shaped block. This was called a sugarloaf. Also, sugar is made from a root vegetable called the sugar beet. The sap of some trees also contains sugar. The sap from the maple tree is made into maple syrup. It is used widely in the United States and Canada on pancakes and waffles.

▼ Herbs are green plants that people use to flavor food. They are used with many kinds of food. For example, many people like mint with lamb, and tarragon with chicken.

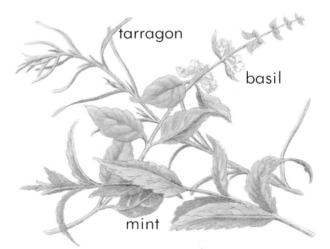

tarragon

basil

mint

▼ This picture shows beekeeping in the Middle Ages. People kept bees in beehives which were woven from grass or rushes, or made from wood. These men have covered their bodies to keep from getting stung. Beekeeping has hardly changed since this picture was painted.

Keeping Food

There are many ways to preserve food and keep it from spoiling. Often, meat and fish were dried out by being covered with salt. Salting food in this way takes out the liquid. This keeps the food from rotting. When the food was to be eaten, it was soaked in water. This washed out much of the salt. Meat and fish can also be stored in a mixture of salt and water called **brine**. When spices are added to brine, it is called **pickling**.

Another way to preserve meat and fish is to salt it and then hang it over a wood fire. The smoke from the fire gives the meat or fish a very good taste. **Smoking** the food preserves it longer than just salting it. Meat, fish, and other foods are also preserved by drying them in the sun or a warm place. Often, fruit, herbs, and mushrooms are dried. Also, fruit is kept by mixing it with a sweetener and boiling the mixture to make jam. That is why jam is sometimes called "preserves."

Canning

Sometimes, food is stored in air-tig cans with oil or brine. The lids are seale onto the cans by a machine. Sometime the cans are put in hot water for sever minutes. This cooks the food insic them. It kills any germs in the food als Food that is stored in cans can be kept fc a very long time.

Canned foods were first used to fee armies of soldiers. In 1809, a Frenchma named Nicholas Appert tried keepir food in bottles. The bottles were seale with corks, and then heated in wate This kept the food free from germs. Bu the bottles were heavy to carry aroun and broke easily.

▼ One way to preserve food is to smoke it. These women are hanging herrings and sardine on sticks. The fish are being carried into the smokehouse to be hung in the smoke above the fire. The smoke changes the taste of the food.

In 1810, an Englishman named Peter urand found out that metal cans could used to preserve food. Cans were uch lighter. He opened the world's first nning factory in 1812. Soon, canned ups and meats went on sale to the blic.

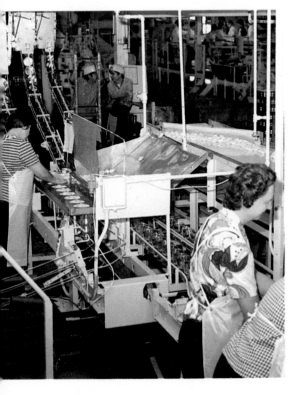

Here, fruit is being canned in the state of regon. Most of the work is done by machines. e women are putting the fruit in the cans. They e checking that the fruit is all right. Syrup is dded and the cans are sealed to keep out the r. Labels are stuck on, and the cans are put in xes.

Food keeps better if it is cool. Before people d refrigerators, they still tried to keep their od cool. Some had iceboxes like this one. thers used cool rooms called larders.

Freezing

Since very early times, people knew that food could be kept if it were stored in cold places. Water, ice, and snow have been used for cooling food since Roman times. Often, food was kept in very cool, dark rooms called **larders**.

Over a hundred years ago, wooden iceboxes were used in Europe to preserve food. Ice was made in a factory and taken to the houses everyday by an iceman. Ice from the United States was even sold to the British in huge blocks. In 1870, the first machines for cooling food were sold. They were called refrigerators.

An American man named Clarence Birdseye found a way of cooling food so much that it is frozen solid. This is called deep-freezing. Food that is deep-frozen can be kept for several months. In 1923, Birdseye set up the first fish-freezing factory in New York. Frozen food is very popular. Many people can now buy and store food in freezers in their homes.

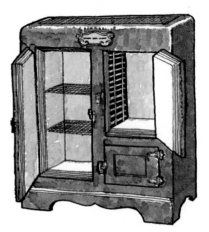

Food and Factories

Today, food in stores is sold in many different ways. Food can be sold in cans, in boxes, or in bottles. Fresh vegetables may only have been picked and washed before being sold. For some foods, there are many different jobs to do before the food can be sold. For almost 200 years, many kinds of food have been prepared and packaged or canned in factories.

Prepared Foods

Today, many foods are prepared, or **processed**, in a factory. Fishcakes, baked beans, or powdered soups are examples of factory-made foods. They are called **convenience foods** because they are ready to eat or only have to be heated up. People can spend less time in the kitchen. These foods can be frozen or kept in cans or boxes for a long time.

▲ People who work cannot always cook their meals. At lunchtime, especially, they may want to buy something ready to eat. They may choose to buy a sandwich, a pie, or a piece of cooked meat.

Some foods cannot be made in a kitchen. They have to be made in a food factory. Many food scientists spend their time in looking for new ways of preparing food or new kinds of food.

An early invention was in 1900. French scientists made something like butter that was cheaper than butter. They found a way to do this in a factory. They used vegetable oils instead of milk. They had made margarine. This could be used instead of butter.

rowing Better Crops

People have always made the soil tter for growing crops by putting imal waste on it. Animal waste that is ed in this way is called **fertilizer**. out a hundred years ago, Sir John nner created another kind of fertilizer. e made this by mixing crushed bones th **minerals** and other materials. day, many farmers use fertilizers and sect killers, called **pesticides**, to oduce better crops. A few farmers do t like using the new fertilizers on food ops. They think that the fertilizers and sticides may harm people. These mers have gone back to the old ways using animal waste. This is called ganic farming**.

Large-Scale Farming

Today, most hens, calves, and pigs do not wander around in open fields or farmyards as they used to do. They are enclosed in small pens or cages with hundreds of others of their kind. This is often called **factory farming**. This way of farming cuts down on the work, and is a cheaper way of producing food. It also produces large amounts of food at one time.

Some people think that this way of farming is cruel. They think that animals should have more space. This would make the food more expensive.

Insects and other pests can destroy crops. rmers may spray their crops to kill the pests. is is a banana plantation in Ecuador. The lds are large and the crops are tall. The siest way to spray them is from an airplane.

▲ People all over the world keep chickens. Often, they are allowed to run loose like these in France. We call chickens that are allowed to do this "free range" chickens. The chickens scratch in the ground to find most of their food. Chickens kept in pens must be fed by the farmer.

Buying and Selling Food

▲ There are open-air markets all over the world. They are held in streets or town squares. People enjoy shopping in them. The food is usually fresh, and the prices are low. This market is in Nigeria.

Food Markets

All over the world, markets were s up where people met to buy and s food. Sometimes, the markets were s up where two roads met, or in th middle of a town. In many countrie street markets still exist. In India, f for example, they are still the mo common place to buy food. In Europe, one time, there were markets that sol one type of food only. You could go fror the Butter Market to the Bread Market.

Food was sold, too, by street sellers, pedlars. They carried the food around i baskets on their heads or slung over the backs. Often, they sold food that the had cooked or picked themselves. To ge people to notice them, they would cr out loudly about what they had to sell.

In the past, people were able to buy food only from farmers or from open stands at a market. In the cities, they could buy from street traders or from small stores. They had to go to a different store for each thing that they wanted. Food did not keep well, so people had to shop everyday. In many places today, people shop only once a week or once a month. They drive to large stores where they can buy everything in one place. Some of these large stores sell mainly food. They are called supermarkets. Other large stores sell clothes, books, toys and many other things as well as food.

ores

Many early food stores were just the
pen fronts of storekeepers' houses. If
e store sold cooked food, it was baked
 the back of the store. The family lived
pstairs.

Often, small villages had just one store
at sold everything from food to clothes
d tools. It was called a General Store.
e different items of food were sold
ose. They were not packaged as they
e today. Sugar, flour, and other goods
ere weighed out into bags by the
orekeeper. There are still stores like this
 small villages all around the world.

Supermarkets

In the early 1900's, an American boy
named Clarence Saunders worked in a
grocery store. People who came to buy
food had to wait while every piece of
food was put on the scales and weighed.
Then, it was wrapped in paper and
priced. Often, there were long lines of
people. Clarence thought that there must
be a better and quicker way to sell food to
people. Why not weigh the food and
wrap it up first? Then, people could help
themselves. In 1919, Clarence opened
the world's first self-service supermarket
in Memphis, Tennessee. The store was
very popular, and now there are
supermarkets all over the world.

Boiled eggs make a very good kind of fast
od. This Chinese picture was painted in China
 the early 1800's. It shows a traveling cook
lling hard-boiled eggs. He uses a boiler to
ok the eggs.

▲ This photograph was taken in 1902. It is the
food department in Macy's department store in
New York City. Today, Macy's is one of the
biggest department stores in the world. It sells
many other things besides food.

Health and Food

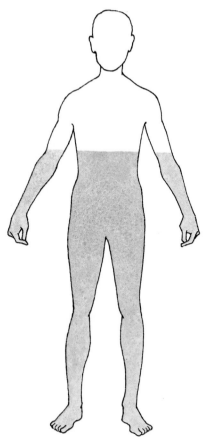

▲ Almost two thirds of the human body is made up of water.

Human bodies must have food and drink before they can work well. Food gives us the energy we require to do our work. Food helps our bodies to grow strong. We could, if we had to, live without any food for several weeks. After that, we would begin to starve. If we do not drink, we cannot stay alive for more than about ten days. This is because almost two thirds of our body is made up of water. We lose some of this water all the time. We must put the water that we lose back into our bodies.

Healthy Eating

Many different types of food are required for good health. Food contains body-building materials. Body-building materials, like **proteins**, are found in foods such as meat, fish, cheese, and nuts. Children need proteins to help them grow. Adults need proteins to repair any damage to their skin or bones. Fruit, dairy foods, vegetables and oil contain vitamins. Vitamins are the materials that help the body to fight against diseases. Foods like bread and rice help to give us energy. Fatty foods, like butter and oils, help to keep us warm. We also need small amounts of different minerals. These are found in many foods.

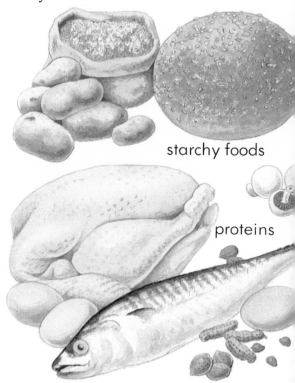

starchy foods

proteins

▲ Each day a person should eat some fruit and vegetables, some starchy food, such as grain or potatoes and some protein.

Unhealthy Eating

People have not always known that they had to eat different types of food to stay healthy. They thought it was good enough to eat any food that filled them up. Many people had crooked bones, bad eyesight, or bad teeth. They did not eat enough of the right kinds of food. They did not store or handle food properly. As a result, men and women often lived only twenty or thirty years. Many children died from diseases before they were five years old. There are still many places where people cannot afford the kind of food they require to stay healthy. They cannot keep food fresh or get clean water. Therefore, many people get sick.

In the past, no one knew that germs live in dirty water and dirty food. These germs cause many diseases. Often, food was stored in dirty pots and touched by unwashed hands. Sometimes, food was mixed with other things that made the food unhealthy. Often, milk was watered down with dirty water. Flour was mixed with chalk.

In many parts of the world, people eat too much and get fat. At one time, people thought that being fat was beautiful. They thought it showed how healthy you were. Today, we know that being too fat is unhealthy. It can put a strain on the heart and other parts of the body.

Fruit and vegetables

▶ Dirty or bad food can make us very sick. It can even kill us. People working with food must keep their hands clean. The equipment they use must also be kept clean.

Hunger and Plenty

In many countries, food crops will grow all through the year. These countries have enough rain to water the crops. They also have enough sunshine, so that the crops will ripen. More food than is required can be grown in these places. There are other countries in the world where it is very hard to grow food. For many months, there may be no rain. A period without rain is called a **drought**. Millions of people and animals die of thirst and hunger during a drought.

Many countries have to grow **cash crops** like tea and coffee. They have t sell these crops to other countries t make money. Often, the cash crops tak up all the farmland. This means foo cannot be grown for the countries' ow people. The people in hot, dry countrie know that rain is not the only way t water crops. They can buy water an pipe it to their land from other place: This is expensive and most of thes countries cannot afford to do this.

▼ Bringing water to dry land is called irrigation. One way to do this is to build ditches through the fields. Water is pumped through them. This irrigation ditch is in Israel.

Too Much Food

In some parts of the world, farmers produce more food than the countries really need. This extra food has to be stored or dumped. In Europe today, there are warehouses and silos full of unused food, like grain, butter, and beef. These are called **food mountains**. If all this food were sold, the prices would be very low. Many farmers would go out of business.

In some parts of the world, people are starving. In other parts of the world, people go on diets because they have too much to eat. People in the past found new ways to grow and transport food. In the same way, people in the future must find new ways to share the world's food, so that no one is hungry.

Where there is no water, food cannot grow nd people may starve. They have to make long urneys to places where they can get food. hese people are in a relief camp in Ethiopia.

rowing Enough Food

Fertilizers are required to grow crops if le land is poor. Often, these come from road and cost a lot of money. Machines ay be needed to help with the work. If le machines break down, there are not ways spare parts for them.

Sometimes, food can be brought into a puntry where the people are starving. his was done in Ethiopia and the Sudan rly in the 1980's. It does not solve the roblem for long. The food from one puntry is not always the kind that eople in another country need. When here is a drought, the problem about rowing food for the next year is still here. The people have to be able to rovide their own food.

▲ In some parts of the world, too much food is produced. The food is often stored in food mountains like this one in Perth, Australia, until it can be used.

43

Quiz

How much can you remember? Try this quiz. Use the glossary and the index to help you find the answers.

1. Here are some names of foods with the letters scrambled. Unscramble them to find the correct names.

   a) OTAPOT, b) THEWA, c) OTAMOT,
   d) YUTREK, e) ECESHE, f) LEPAINEPP

2. Which is the odd one out?

   a) vitamins, minerals, proteins, germs
   b) yam, coffee, ale, tea
   c) canning, smoking, freezing, planting
   d) wheat, cheese, corn, rice
   e) molasses, honey, herbs, sugar

3. Complete the following sentences with (a), (b), (c) or (d).

   1) A metal cooking pot, used for boiling water, is called
      a) a crop.
      b) a range.
      c) a spit.
      d) a cauldron.

   2) A chappatti is
      a) a kind of pasta, eaten in Italy.
      b) a kind of cake, eaten in Austria.
      c) a kind of bread, eaten in India.
      d) a kind of fish, caught in Japan.

   3) Chopsticks are
      a) street sellers.
      b) needed for good health.
      c) sticks used to pick up food.
      d) small pots used for cooking.

   4) Halal meat is eaten by people of
      a) the Jewish religion.
      b) the Christian religion.
      c) the Buddhist religion.
      d) the Muslim religion.

   5) Jethro Tull invented
      a) the combine harvester.
      b) the plough.
      c) the hoe.
      d) the seed drill.

   6) A drought is
      a) a machine for taking weeds out of the soil.
      b) a shortage of rain.
      c) a disease caused by lack of vitamin C.
      d) a wild grass seed.

4. These words have been written backwards. Can you see what they are? Which five help to flavor foods?

   a) SNIARG, b) SECIPS, c) SESSALOM,
   d) HSERHT, e) SBREH, f) YENOH,
   g) SELKCIS, h) REDRAL, i) TLAS,
   j) OOBMAB

5. Are these statements true or false?
   a) People used to eat swans and peacocks.
   b) Grains are grown on trees.
   c) Fish can be frozen on board a ship.
   d) Citrus fruits contain a lot of vitamin C
   e) Sugar grows both above and below the ground.
   f) It does not cost a lot of money to pipe water from one country to another.

There are two men in this book who have the first name of Clarence. Give their full names and say what each of them did.

What is
a) a pedlar?
b) a hypermarket?
c) cinnamon?
d) Thanksgiving Day?
e) Diwali?

Which of the following events took place first?
a) Explorers from Europe set out to look for other lands.
b) People hunted for food and only ate it raw.
c) People learned to fish and trap birds.
d) Extra food is stored in food mountains.

e) Fish shops in Britain were opened.

9. Where
a) were sausages known over 3,000 years ago.
b) were machines first used to cut the crops?
c) were the first turkeys found?
d) did people first find a way to thicken milk to make yogurt?
e) are cormorants used to catch fish?

10. Match the words below to one of these four groups:

**fish   vegetables   milk
grains**

cheese, corn, rice, carrots, yams, curds, cod, garum

ANSWERS

1. a) POTATO, b) WHEAT, c) TOMATO, d) TURKEY, e) CHEESE, f) PINEAPPLE

2. (a) germs (all the others are body-building substances), (b) yam (all the others are drinks), (c) planting (all the others are ways of preserving), (d) cheese (all the others are types of grain), (e) herbs (all the others are sweeteners)

3. 1 (d), 2 (c), 3 (c), 4 (d), 5 (d), 6 (b)

4. b) SPICES, c) MOLASSES, e) HERBS, f) HONEY, i) SALT

5. a) true, b) false, c) true, d) true, e) true, f) false

6. Clarence Birdseye opened the first factory for deep-freezing fish.

7. a) A pedlar was a travelling salesman. b) A hypermarket is a large self-service store that sells food and other goods such as clothes. c) Cinnamon is a spice. d) Thanksgiving is a celebration held in the United States on the fourth Thursday in November. e) Diwali is a festival held in India.
Clarence Saunders opened the first supermarket.

8. b)

9. a) Babylon, b) United States, c) South America, d) Turkey, e) Japan and China

10. **fish** - cod, garum **vegetables** - yams, carrots **milk** - cheese, curds **grains** - rice, corn

Glossary

bake oven: a pan with a lid which was used for cooking bread.

blowpipe: a long, straight tube from which an arrow or dart can be blown. Often, it is made from a plant stalk.

breed: to produce young. Some people breed animals by choosing adults which are special. They may be strong, or fast, or attractive.

brine: water that has a lot of salt in it. Brine is used for preserving food.

can: (1) to store in sealed metal containers . (2) a container made of metal in which food and liquids can be sealed for storage.

cash crop: a crop that people grow to sell rather than use themselves.

cassava: also called manioc. A tropical plant with a thick root. A flour is made from the root.

cauldron: a large kettle or pot for boiling or heating liquids.

cereal: a grass plant that produces seeds that can be eaten. Wheat, rice, millet, and sorghum are cereals.

chappatti: a thin, flat bread which is made in India. Chappattis are made from flour and water, and cooked on a flat pan.

chili: powder made from dried red chili peppers. It is very hot and strong.

chopsticks: two thin sticks about ten inches long, which are made of wood or ivory. They are used by the people of Asia to pick up food, instead of a knife and fork.

churn: to shake or stir vigorously. Milk is churned to separate the fat to make butter.

cinnamon: a yellow-brown powder that is made from the bark of a tree which grows in Sri Lanka. Cinnamon is used to flavor food.

cistern: a large tank for storing water.

citric acid: a sour-tasting acid. Citric acid is found in large amounts in citrus fruits like lemons.

combine harvester: a moving machine that cuts cereals and separates the grain from the straw.

convenience food: food that is partly made or cooked before it is sold. It is much quicker and easier to prepare than ordinary food.

crop: plants, such as grain, fruit, or vegetables grown by people for food.

crystal: a substance which has many sides. Some liquids form crystals when cooled or boiled.

curd: the thick part of milk. The curd separate out from the liquid when the milk turns sour.

dairy food: the different kinds of food like butter and cheese which come from milk.

drought: a long time without rain.

factory farming: a way of farming where lots c the same kind of animal are kept crowded together. The animals are specially fed, so that they produce more food.

fertilizer: a substance which is added to the so to make plants grow well.

food mountain: a very large amount of food that is being stored until it is needed. Food mountains occur when more food than can be eaten is produced.

garum: a mixture made from fish which the Romans used to add flavor to their food.

germ: a very tiny living thing that can cause diseases. Germs can be seen only with a very strong microscope.

ghee: butter which has been heated and cooled Ghee keeps better than fresh butter. It is often made from buffalo milk.

grain: a small, hard seed from a kind of grass.

grind: to crush and rub something to make a fine powder.

halal: to kill an animal in a special way. Halal killing follows the rules of the Muslim religion.

hoe: (1) to scrape, dig, or loosen the soil, so tha weeds and stones can be removed (2) a long-handled tool with a small blade that is used for loosening the soil.

hop: a climbing plant. Its bitter cone-shaped fruits are used to flavor beer.

invention: something that has not been designed or made before.

sher: a special way of killing animals and preparing meat that follows the rules of the Jewish religion.

der: a small room or cabinet, usually with an hole, where food can be kept cool and fresh.

llstone: one of the two stones which rub ether to crush grains to make flour.

neral: natural substances that have not been med from plant or animal life. Rocks, metals, d salt are minerals. Anything which grows in soil takes in minerals through its roots.

chi: a soft paste made from beating rice and ter together. Mochi is eaten in Japan.

lasses: a thick, sweet, dark brown liquid. lasses can be drained from raw sugarcane.

hard: a piece of land that is used to grow it trees.

anic farming: a method of farming which es not use fertilizers or insect killers made from emicals.

ssover: a yearly Jewish festival. Passover is a e when the escape of the Jews from slavery in ypt is celebrated.

dlar: a person who goes from place to place ling things.

sticide: a chemical which kills insects and sts.

kle: to preserve food in a special liquid, like egar or salt water.

llen: the tiny grains or "dust" found in wers. Pollen helps to make seeds.

ultry: birds such as hens or ducks which are pt for eggs and meat.

eserve: to keep from spoiling. Food can be eserved in several ways.

ocessed: treated or prepared by several ferent actions.

otein: an important substance found in foods ch as meat, fish, eggs, cheese, and beans.

nge: a large, flat-topped kitchen stove. It is de of metal, and contains a fire which heats e oven and hot plates.

ap: to cut and gather a cereal crop.

e: a grass-like plant. Its seed is used for king bread.

settle: to stay in one place to make a home.

sickle: a tool with a long curved blade and short handle that is used for cutting crops or grass.

sift: to separate small pieces from large pieces by passing them through a net or sieve.

smoke: a way of preserving and flavoring food by cooking it in smoke.

spit: a metal rod on which food can be put and then cooked over a flame. Spits usually have a handle, so that the food can be turned.

staple: the food which makes up the biggest part of everything that a person eats.

strudel: a type of pastry. It is rolled out until it is paper thin.

sugarcane: a tall, woody grass that grows in tropical places. Sugarcane is the plant from which most of our sugar comes from.

tea-caddy: an airtight box for holding tea leaves.

temple: a building made for the worship of a god or gods.

thresh: to beat or thrash crops such as wheat or rice in order to make the grain fall off the stalk.

trade: to buy and sell goods.

trawl: to fish with a big net which is pulled along by a fishing boat.

tropical: from the tropics which are part of the world near or at the equator. The tropics are hot and damp.

vegetarian: a person who does not eat meat. Vegetarians eat mainly vegetable food.

vine: a climbing plant that produces grapes.

vitamin C: a substance which is found in foods such as fresh vegetables and fruit. Vitamin C is important for good health.

whey: the watery pale part of milk. When milk is churned or turns sour, the whey separates out from the fattier part.

yam: a root-vegetable that grows in hot climates.

yeast: a yellowish substance made up of very tiny plants. Yeast grows quickly and gives off gas when it is warmed. It is used to make bread rise and for making beer and wine.

yogurt: milk that has been thickened to become almost solid by adding enzymes.

Index

LOO
   Looking back at food
   and drink

DATE DUE			